A TALE OF A MARRIED WOMAN

CURSE, DOWRY, HATRED- DOES ANJANA DESERVE THESE? KNOW IN THIS PART OF THE STORY

RANA RASHID

ISBN 979-888606280-9

This book is strongly dedicated to all lovely and strong women in the world who despite of facing several ups and down in their life, mentally & physically being hurt by their in-laws never complained anyone how they feel from inside. A great salute to them!

I also dedicate this book to all professionals who holds the pride to the profession by printing and selling this book.

Last but not the least, I dedicate this book to my parents who have been continuously by my side making me morally strong in every possible way they can.

Contents

Preface

So long you have ambitions, nothing can drag you back

It is said that men are stronger than women. But, those who says have ever thought that if a woman has the power to give a human being, then she has been blessed with the God's power to overcome anything in her life. The only need is to feel your inner power without giving the command button in someone else's hand.

What kind of book is it?

'A Tale of a Married Woman' Part I book is something that not only describes the life of a character but nearly 80% of the women and their families in the world faces the same situation after marriage. This book is medium for every woman to relate her life and feel it deeply.

Will its Part II be available?

Yes, this book has the Part II that will be releasing very soon.

Acknowledgements

I thank my mom & dad who has always been standing as a strong pillar beside my side. With their moral support, I could make myself to take up any challenge in my life.

I thank my sister who has always been a guide in my life, helping me to push myself in challenging situations.

I lastly thank to all negative persons in my life whose negativities inspired me to write this book and make myself a worth valuing.

It is not possible to give credit to each one separately, so I express my gratitude to everyone whoever have directly or indirectly contributed to this work.

Prologue

Part I 'A Tale of a Married Woma' is a story of a 25 years old lady, Anjana who got married to a family where she has to face several ups and downs. She is a bit anguished, but still manage to find happiness in a tough situation. The demand of dowry from her in-laws at the last moment left her with no option to accept or reject the proposal. She was completely clueless when her parents received a call from her to be in-laws just a day before the marriage to come up and deliver the hefty amount asap or else the groom won't visit the bride's place for marriage. Will Anjana be happy to her in-law's place after fulfilling the demand of those greedy family or she will still continue to suffer?

CHAPTER ONE

A Saga of An Arranged Marriage

Rrrrrr.....phone rings

"Hello mumma... Yes, I'm back from office".

"Yes I already had my dinner". What about you?

Is it possible to take few days leave and come home?- Mom on other side of call.

"What happen mumma?"

"See, we are very much worried about your marriage. If you stay such a far away from us giving excuse of job everytime, then, how we will be able to find a guy for you?"

She sighs, " Not again please". Last month only I visited home. I can't take off again. Why don't you convince the guy to meet over here?

See dear, You have to understand this. It's a very crucial time, and you have to cooperate with the situation. If taking leave is such a problem, then, why don't you resign and come back home?

Mumma please, let me think about it. Chalo, I am very tired now. Going to have my dinner, Bye!

Call disconnected.....

Arranged marriages in Indian society are way long and complicated procedure. No matter whether a girl is literate or illiterate, she has to pass in multiple stages of the face showing rituals. Sometimes, she gets rejected just because she is way high literate than a guy, sometimes gets rejection just because her education doesn't match the guy's literacy, or sometimes the proposal is so pathetic that she has no choice but to reject it. If I compare this with applying for a job procedure, don't you think that both have similarities? In the case of jobs, most of the time you get rejected because either your qualification and experience don't match the job profile or sometimes you reject the opportunity because you think that the job profile is too low as per your experience. Isn't it?

Well, let me stick to the arranged marriage. The girls' decisions to tie a knot with someone solely depends on how much does the families like each other, what is the earnings of the prospective grooms and bride, and in some of the fortunate cases the opinions of the would-be bride and groom.

This story is of two characters whose solder was just a destiny call. Anjana, a girl of middle-class working family whose ambitions is to fly high in the sky with her wings spread wide, while Amreet is a guy of a struggling family whose childhood has passed completely different from other kids and whose bachelorette has driven him to struggle vigorously to earn livelihood.

Anjana, a 25 years old girl belongs to a family who always wanted their daughter to study and become independent. Anjana's family comprises of two daughters and a younger son. Her family was not only modern but, an open-minded who thinks that boys and girls are all same and so is their upbringings. Her family never discriminated among son and daughter and equally gave them education. So, most of her bachelorette was spent studying far away from her hometown. She pursued her Master's degree from Bangalore, engrossed herself as a trainee for testing medicines for cancer in research institute, and finally stepped into a medical writing job in a private company. Days passed by and her job life was running with full-fledge with no worries and no tension. But being a young and beautiful lady, she also has weaved dreams for her marriage, where her prince charm will come and will hold her hand. One thing that definitely every girl wants that she wouldn't be the burden for her dad. And so was Anjana! She always wanted to marry someone who has the guts to take the responsibility and sole decision and not the one who only remains as a puppet for his parents.

However, the search was in continuation. Her parents were looking for a perfect match for more than 2 years and hence, due to above said formalities, she was yet to meet her Mr. Perfect. Yes, destiny has planned for her and she was waiting for it to get it to unfold.

Here's her parent's search ends....

Anjana's father was approached by a guy through a matrimonial site and surprisingly everything seems perfect. She was insisted by her parents to meet the guy once, as both of them were living in the same city. One night her dad called up and said, "Beta, did u check the guy's photo? I have texted you."

Anjana: Papa, did you find the guy suitable?

Dad: yes, he seems perfect for us.

Anjana: where's mummy? Let me ask her. She will explain to me much better.

Dad handed over the mobile to Mom

Mumma, how do you take up this guy? Is he having moustache?

Mumma: Laughs! Arey no... Don't worry. He is a clean shave. By the way, he wants to have a meeting with you. So, will you be able to meet up on Sunday?

Anjana: Fine! But, ask him to call me before 8 PM. After that I won't pick call

Anjana's dad shared her no. to the guy. One day before the meeting, the guy called her:

Hi!

Hello! who's this?

Guy! I got your number from your dad. Is this Anjana speaking?

Yes speaking, please tell me (Anjana already got to know that this was the same guy about which her parents were talking about). But, she pretended to be unknown.

Ohh yeah! Please tell me..

Can we have a meeting on Sunday? You decide the spot and we'll meet there., if you don't mind.

No that's fine. Dad already told me about the meeting.

Conversation ended.....

On a very fine day, both of them decided to meet at a decided place.

With excitement to meet someone who might be your prince charm, Anjana engrossed herself in choosing her outfit. She dressed up nicely and looked at the mirror twice and thrice to crosscheck whether everything is perfect. Isn't the colour of the lipstick very dark? Am I looking gorgeous? These questions were arising in her mind. Well, it's now time to head out for the decided place.

Anjana: Hi! Where are you? I reached

Guy on another side of call: Oh! Ok.. Just about to reach. Actually, got stuck in traffic

Anjana thinks "can't he come earlier?" Don't know how long he's gonna make me wait here.

The only problem was with her that she was worried about whether her hair doesn't get tangled, and her face doesn't look weird due to sweating. She only wants to look perfect on her first meeting.

Finally, she could see a guy approaching her.

Sky-blue jeans complimenting a checked shirt, and glass on the face. His index finger moving a car key and eyes eagerly searching here and there for someone.

But, oh, who is he? He was followed by another guy who has noticed her before him. With a smile on his face, he whispered something to Amreet. He was Amreet's close friend.

Well, finally they both met and decided to sit and talk at Mc Donald's restaurant. With a bit of shyness, eagerness, and mixed feelings of nervousness, both had a good time over the conversation, taking a sip of cold coffee together, while his friend ordered french fries. The normal conversation ended with a laughter and fun. Though the conversation was normal, but, there was several minute and important things that each one of them were trying to understand. For example, whether Anjana will work or not after marriage? Does she will stay as a housewife if asked to? and alot more.

The guy as he seemed to be was exactly the same. He made Anjana completely comfortable and this was the reason, both talked to each other openly.

Finally, it was time to leave.

Guy: How will you go?

Anjana: I will be taking an auto from here. It was nice meeting you, she smiled.

He smiles and with some doubt, asked. "If you don't mind, shall I drop you"?

She was a bit confused, but, later on, agreed.

On her entire way, Anjana thinks, "Oh God, when will I reach? Why the route seems so long?" I hope this feeling has happened with every girl when she is accompanied by someone unknown.

Finally, she was back in her lounge!

Hello papa, I'm back.

How was your meeting? Anjana's parents asked?

Nice!

I am very tired papa. Going to take a nap. Bye, will talk in the evening.

After she woke up in the evening, she picked up her mobile to check. She has received a message from the guy mentioning that "I reached my room".

Hastily, she woke up on the bed and unlocked her mobile to check the message.

By the time she was just checking, the guy called up. Hi! You didn't even ask me whether have I reached my place or not?

A rush of blood flows down her spine. She smiled

I am sorry, I didn't ask you. Actually, I fall asleep. Thought will call you after I woke up.

Ohh.. Don't lie. You wouldn't have called me if I haven't called you up.

Both smiled.

And the conversation lasted for a minute or two.

The guy was well-educated and has no such expectations. On the other hand, both the families bonded in such a way that they knew each other. She met the guy twice before marriage and a string of attachment and emotions have started creating among them. Whenever they used to meet each other, the guy always tried to explain more and more about his family, his mom-dad, sisters and her kids. Though it was very golden and romantic period so Anjana used to think that she was quite smart to handle his family wisely.

Time passed by, the message conversation was then transformed into the Whatsapp conversation and both chatted lately. And finally, both of them decided that they must marry together.

CHAPTER TWO

A Month Before Marriage....

As both the couple has known each other, it was the time for both the families to know each other and see the girl and guy from themselves. So, a date was decided when Anjana's parents were going to visit the guy's place. They wanted to meet his family, check the house where they are supposed to send their daughter, in-laws behavior, and lots more. As soon as Anjana's parents, sister, and her brother reached, they were impressed with the first sight of the place. They were extremely happy to see. They were welcomed inside the house where the guys' parents, and sisters were already present. With lots of discussions and meeting the guy, Anjana's parents were satisfied with the relation.

Now the turn was the guy's family to visit Anjana's place. Today his family was arriving. So, a lot of preparation was going on. Anjana and her mom was busy in kitchen. Her brother was busy in managing house, sister was busy in taking care of all the things properly, while her dad was ready to welcome them at the society gate. Finally, they arrived. The guests were accompanied by Anjana's dad inside the room. Mom made them sit comfortably and take rest. Then, lots of dishes were served in front of them. Now, Anjana was called to come in front of the guests *"As every Indian tradition happens (Munh dekhai)"*. She was sitting on the chair in front of everyone and the guests were continuously starring at her. She was asked few questions from them and finally Anjana passed.

After they all had lunch, it was now the time to set the date of marriage. And here the situation takes a U-turn. The guy's sister whispered something to her mom's ears and then something happened that no one in Anjana's family was expecting. They have a demand of dowry. *(Yes, you heard it right. A demand of a hefty amount.)*

The guy's dad said to Anjana's mom and dad that we want around 7 lakhs cash along with a car and rest all that you want to give your daughter. Hearing this the family got stunned, speechless. As if the ground has slipped under their feet. And the last statement from the guy's dad was that "We won't fix the date now. You have to come again to our house with final consent. If you agree on this, then we can fix the date of marriage". Finally, the guests left.

The Moment of happiness was drastically turned into a tension. But, still Anjana's parents decided that we must visit the place once again. Let's put our word and will see what happen. And on a very fine day they visited to the guy's place once again. As per the tradition, Anjan's parents were carrying to be son in-law's dress, shoes, grooming kit, sweets, a gold ring as a gift. But, when they arrived their house, Anjana's mom instructed their driver to take care of the gifts until she asks him to carry those gifts inside. They then went inside the house where they were made seated. But, this time unfortunately the mood of the guys' family was not good as before. And the discussion started. The greedy in-laws put their words before Anjan's parents that we will proceed further with the dates only when our demand will get fulfilled. They were not even ready to compromise. Anjan's mom was short tempered. So, without eating anything she hastily get up from the couch and said, "I am not ready to give my daughter to these greedy people". Anjan's sister tried convincing her mom, but she didn't agree. And left the house with tears and anger.

When they all came back, Anjana excitedly asked, "Mom, how was the discussion?" What did they say?

Mom: Anjana, I don't like this family at all. They are very greedy. You just forget the guy.

Anjana: Mom, Call them and just try to convince them.

No, I don't even like to talk to them.

Anjana: You talk dad, if possible.

Anjana's dad was in dilemma. He wasn't able to understand what to do. Finally, he decided to call the guy's dad.

Hello, the guy's dad on the other side of the call. Yes tell me.

Anjana's dad: I won't be able to give you such a big amount. It's completely impossible for me to arrange.

Guy's dad: Then, forget about this marriage. You call me only when you are able to arrange.

Anjana's dad: Please reduce the amount. Because, it's about happiness of both kids

Guy's dad: It won't be less than 4 lakhs. Or else just end this up.

Anjana's dad really wanted to end this up with those greedy people. But, Anjana's happiness was adhered with it. S, finally he agreed.

Ok, I will be giving you 4 lakhs. But, it will be in cheque.

Guy's dad: No no, not in cheque. give me cash and send me before marriage.

Her dad was left with no other option. So, finally he started arranging the amount. He arranged only 2 lakhs for now. One month before marriage her dad went with 2 lakh cash. He reached to the guy's place and handed over the amount to his dad. As soon as he left the house, a news got spread. And that was "The prime minister has announced the demonetization (note ban). This shooked everyone's head, and so the guy's family too. Because, the amount was full of 1000 and 500 notes.

Dear readers, see the cunningness of the guy's family.

As soon as the Anjana's dad returned back home, he got a call from the guy's dad saying that, "Take all your amount back, as it is of no use due to demonetizaton." Now, Anjana's mom took the phone from her dad and spoke rudely. She said, "listen to me very carefully. My husband has already handed over you the amount. And the news has spread just after he left your house. So, those amounts are not our responsibility, but, it's yours. Now, do whatever you want with those amounts. Burn it, flow it, or threw it. But, don't call us again for this."

The marriage date was approaching nearby, just a month was left and a lot was still pending. In those hectic moment, both the couple were still in touch. However, both of them decided to enjoy shopping together. So, these love birds took out special two-three days from their busy professional schedule and started visiting showrooms. Sometimes for lehengas, and sometimes for sherwanis. Somehow, both of them managed to fulfil the major requirements, and the rest was left on their parents.

One night over phone call....

12.04 AM: Phone rings.. Anjana picks the call.

Amreet: Hey which place would you like to visit after marriage?

Anjana: Mmmmm. Not sure... U decide..

I am finalizing Andaman, Amreet said.. Will that be fine?

Wow amazing.. Are you sure? Will we be visiting Andaman after marriage?

Yes, baba. Let me look into the package.. Will send you few of the selected package. Just finalise one of them.

Sure! Anjana excitedly replied.

Just a day after...

Anjana received a message from Amreet. Seeing the message, she lost her control and jumped up the bed. Guess what? It was nothing but a booking for the Andaman.

Hastily, she picked up her mobile and dialed Amreet's number.. Finally, we are going? I can't imagine... Really love u a lot. This is the statement that came for the first time from her side.

Anjana was working in an MNC in a metro city. But, as her date of marriage was approaching, she has to resign from the job and return to her hometown, because very few days were left and still lots of work was pending. However, she got occupied in finalizing her outfit, her makeup, jewelry, and lots more that she hardly got time to chat with the guy now. Her parents were engrossed in deciding venues, catering, guest lists, as well as gifts. But, the image of Amreet was always in front of her eyes and on her mind (Have

I mentioned the guy's name anywhere?). Well, Amreet was his soulmate or you can say her prince charm. All she dreamt of spending a queen lifestyle with him, with no worries, no boundaries. Just a life where friendship and romance have maximum dominancy.

Today, Anjana's parents were coming to pick her up. This was just because it was very tough for her to carry entire all her own to her hometown. Actually, she was leaving her working city, her Pg. Her sister Gracy who was residing with her was coming along. She was also engrossed in packing with her sister. Finally, they all were set to leave for the station. Undoubtedly, the entire family was filled with joy and excitement. They were seen taking selfies, gossiping about arrangements and lots more.

They all reached the railway station 1 hour before. Tired yet excited, they sat down somewhere in the vacant place. In the meantime Anjana received a call from Amreet.

Amreet: Did u reach the railway station?

Yes we are here, Anjana replied! Are you in office?

No, I am on the way. I am coming to visit you and mumma, papa.

Anjana: Arey, no. Why are you coming? It will be hectic for you.

That's fine. We have almost reached. I am with my friend. And listen, I have packed dinner with me. Just tell me where are you.

Anjana: Ok. Just give me a call as soon as you reach on the overhead bridge. I'll come there itself.

Finally, they met each other. Amreet handed her bag of dinner and then left from there.

....

Anjana's house started getting crowded with her relatives. Her mama, mami, cousins, and everyone has arrived.

Just one day before marriage, a proper ritual that happens in every Indian family was Haldi and Mehendi function. Anjana's hands and feet were embellished with beautiful designs of henna. While on the other side Amreet was also busy looking after all the preparations as well as he was also being engaged in applying Haldi. But, despite all the gatherings and family clutters, the romance of these love birds was at the highest peak. They didn't leave a single opportunity to click their Mehendi and share with each other.

In such a happy and joyful moment, Anjana's dad gort a call from her in-laws asking for the rest of the 2 lakhs. Amreet's brother on the other side of the call, "Uncle, we want rest of the 2 lakhs or else we won't come with the bride." Anjana's dad was completely tensioned. He couldn't think what to do now. He didn't even want to create a scene. So, he said please trust me, I will give the rest of the amount soon as lots of money has been drained in arranging the marriage. But, Amreet's family on the other side was not ready to negotiate. And at the last, Anjana's dad came to a conclusion that he will be giving rest of the 2 lakhs in cheque as soon as the bride and guests will be arriving. They finally then agree.

Finally, the date of marriage has come, and Anjana was all set to become the lady of his dream. The function was solemnized grandiosely and it was now the time for the girl to say farewell to her parents. In Hindi, we call it Bidai ceremony. I hope, this is the most heart-breaking time when a girl has to leave a parent's house to settle down with someone to some place where she is completely unknown. But, what to do? It's something that every Indian girl has to follow custom, and so did Anjana. She broke down with tears when she hugged her dad, as she never knew that it would pain so much when she has to leave her lovable mom and dad.

Finally, she was at Amreet's place where her mother-in-law and other relatives were waiting for several rituals to perform. Everything was new for her, but, yes quite happening and full of excitement. Lots of fun and frolic giggle talks were there, and she was the center of attraction for everyone over there.

CHAPTER THREE

A Day in Amreet's House...

The next morning when she woke up, everything was new for her. New room, new people around, new environment, and new talks. Something that was not with her was her daddy's routine of listening to television in full volume, her mumma's shouting to get up early in the morning and have breakfast, her brother's tease, and lots more. Seems, she was missing all of these.

But, she got blenched when she heard her mother-in-law shouting on her bhabhi for not taking pallu on her head. Not only her mother-in-law, but, even younger sister of Amreet was also involved in back biting. She has never undergone these kinds of situation, so she got bit nervous.

She freshened up herself and got ready as a new bride. Neighbours were continuously coming to look at her as if she was something like an antique piece. Anyways, a new bride is always an antique piece for every new person. So, she had no choice but to greet each and everyone with a smiling face.

Hope many of you have experienced those ladies when they come to see a new bride and makes them uncomfortable. The same happened to Anjana.

Lady in Neighbourhood: Where is Bahu?

Mother-in-law: She is in her room. Go and see her.

Anjana can hear the voice of her mother-in-law. So, she prepared herself to meet the lady. Took pallu on her head and sat quietly.

The door opened; someone was peeping from the curtain. Anjana could see her and with her smiling face, she greeted her and welcomed her in the room and to sit beside her.

Now, imagine how you feel when there is no topic for conversation and someone keeps starring at you continuously. The same happened with Anjana.

This lady was looking at her. Sometimes, her face, and sometimes her dress. May be some chemical turmoil was going on in her mind. Anjana with her eyes down can see all these and was feeling very uncomfortable. She was wishing for someone to call this lady outside, as the aura of the room was very tensed.

Finally, she managed to get rid of her. Same day evening, some of Amreet's friends visited his house. Amreet called Anjana to joined them. And the evening was spent with lots of giggling. Overall, the day was very tiring for her.

The only reason why people were so eagerly visiting the place was that the couple had already planned an outing on the third day after marriage. And the trip was for more than a week. Well, now Anjana has to pack her luggage as they have to leave for a trip the next day. She was very excited as this was the first time, she was visiting with her hubby.

CHAPTER FOUR

Amreet Finally Resumes His Office..

Finally, after 1 month of marriage, the couple had to depart from their family members as there was a shortage in Amreet's leave.

Amreet's same old routine started, but, something new that was added to his life was Anjana's presence. As compared to before, Amreet seems more enthusiastic, energetic as well as happy. The first day in his office was passing in hardship, as he was waiting to come home as early as possible where he could meet his lovely wife. While, on the other hand, Anjana's day was spent arranging the house and organizing each and everything.

The clock struck 6 in the evening and Anjana dressed up herself with her eyes all set to look for her hubby.

The doorbell rings, Anjana hastily opened up the door, and guess who? It was none other than Amreet. A smile flashed on both faces and both of them hugged each other.

Amreet kept his bag, changed his cloth, and walked towards the washroom to freshen up himself.

Something delicious was waiting for him, as Anjana has cooked special mutton curry with his favorite delicacy i.e. kheer. Both had a good time over dinner.

Days passed by, and the same routine was being followed by both of them.

2 Years passed of their marriage...

Anjan called him and burst, "When are you coming home?"

"I will be late. Have dinner sweetie."

"Don't call me sweetie! This is 3rd time this week! If I had to eat my dinner alone, I could have done at my mom's house also!" fulminated, she disconnected.

He sighed. Two years of marriage and she still wanted all the attention.

Amreet- I didn't remember when was the last time I hang out with 'the guys'. After slogging the entire week at the office, today I secretly wanted to, but not at the cost of making her upset. Amreet thinks.

Amreet called her: Don't be angry, we will go out for dinner tomorrow?

Anjana: :(

Amreet: I am really, really stuck in traffic.

Anjana: :(:(

Amreet: Okay we will go out today

Anjana: I will be ready in an hour. thank you sweetie :)

'Don't call me sweetie' Amreet wanted to remind her. But he didn't.

On their way to the restaurant, she insisted to go to the outskirts. 1.5-hour drive from home. Amreet couldn't refuse. Five minutes into their journey and her mother call up.

"Hello Mumma!" she hooted.

"Yes we are going somewhere," she added.

"No No, he takes good care of me." she laughed.

"Really!" Anjana turns to me to inform, "Gracy got engaged." and continues to get details from her mum.

And so, the only unmarried and cute sister-in-law is also officially off the flirt-me zone. So, no unmarried sisters-in-law? And I am going to celebrate- Amreet thinks

For the 40-45 minutes, mother-daughter continue their conversation with least bother about her husband driving listening to FM, feeling left out. –

"Where are we?" - Anjana asked

"NH-8, we will reach Gurgaon shortly.." - Amreet replied

"Why are you being so silly! We should have been driving to Mumma's place!" - Anjana curiously said.

"But you said you had to dine at..." Amreet grinned.

"Gracy is getting engaged and you think we will go to some restaurant?? What is the matter with you??" - Anjana said

What am I supposed to do if I can't read clues? How would I know if she's getting engaged right now? Amreet thought. He quietly went off the highway looking for a u-turn.

After another exhaustive drive of an hour, Anjana somehow reach her maternal place. Thank God for lesser-than-usual traffic today. Once there, they were all standing outside to welcome them.

Amreet- "Namaste mummy-ji" and bowed down to take her blessings. Sister-in-law is standing right there and came to half-hug me.

"So Gracy finally found your prince eh?" Amreet teased her.

Anjana pulled her away from Amreet and soon disappeared inside the house. He don't have to do much, except smile at them purposelessly.

At 12.30 in the night, they finally board their car to go back home.

"After Gracy will also go away, mom-dad will be all alone" Anjana started shedding tears.

'Their responsibilities will be over, they might be happy' Amreet wanted to tell her. But, couldn't.

"Gracy will be happy with him," Amreet told her.

Anjana- "I wish he will be as good as you." she stopped crying and told Amreet.

By applying semi-brakes to the car, Amreet turned to her and said, "Wow. You think I am good?"

"You are the best. The best companion one could ever hope for!" - Anjana replied

Amreet- "Really you mean it? I mean, the way our day went, it is hard to imagine this coming from you." Amreet smiled.

Anjana- "I have only you to complain, to fight with, and to cry in front of. If I do all this, it doesn't mean my love for you is getting any lesser. It only increases as I see you come home skipping all appointments, drive for 2-2 hours tirelessly, and then behave so nicely to make me happy and fulfilling all my desires."

CHAPTER FIVE

Desire or Demand of Happiness

Being a woman, each one of you might have experienced once in your life the joy of getting pregnant for the first time. Knowingly or unknowingly this phase comes in every married woman's life. Anjana was too eagerly waiting for this precious moment to come into her life. One evening when both were somewhere out in the car, Anjana asked Amrit

"Can we have a baby?"

Are you serious? I think we should take some more time, Amreet said.

But, don't you feel that we require someone who could add a bundle of joy to our life, Anjana uttered this sentence demandingly.

Amreet smiled at her and finally, the topic seemed to be paused at this time.

One morning when Anjana was on a call with her mother-in-law, something she got to know that made her a bit anguished.

Can't you come before so that you can engross yourself in chores? mom-in-law on another side.

Yes Maa, we are trying too. Although, Amreet is struggling to get leave.

Don't you have a commonsense that my daughter is still managing all household chores. If she still continues working then, definitely the color of henna is not going to get darker on her rough hands.

Shockingly, Anjana uttered just one word "OK"

Call Disconnected

What was the stupidity? I never heard this before. Even after resigning from my job, I was helping my mom with all household chores for one month. Despite that, my henna got darker. Anjana thought.

The harsh voice of Amreet's mom for the first time when she heard made Anjana upset but didn't reveal it in front of Amreet.

It was Anjana's sister-in-law's marriage, so both were desperately busy shopping. Hence, the topic was skipped out of their mind.

Next day morning:

Sunday 11 AM

Anjana: Wake up Amreet, It's already 11 o'clock. Our train is at 4 PM. Hurry up or we'll get late. Check whether all packings are done perfectly or anything still left. I am going to the kitchen

Saying this, Anjana hastily headed towards the kitchen and got busy herself preparing and packing dishes for the journey.

"Oh, I forgot to mention that both the couple has to leave for their hometown today, as Amreet's younger sister is getting married".

A Voice from the kitchen ushered to Amreet's ear- Amreet, you are definitely going to make us late. Please wake up and get ready.

Amreet's all of a sudden woke up and checked time, Oh My God, it's already 12 PM.

Anjana, have you completed all your chores? Anyhow, we have to leave for the railway station by 2.45, then only we can reach on time. I am going to take bath. In the mean-time please wrap up everything.

"Actually, the most important thing that every girl gets worried about while traveling is that nothing should she forget, right from her favorite dress to her make-up."

Anjana was also checking whether she has kept all her cosmetics as well as jewelry or not.

Finally, they both reached the railway station.

After two months of their marriage, Anjana was visiting her in-law's house for the first time. So, undoubtedly, she was nervous yet excited.

On their way to complete the journey, Amreet kept explaining everything about his family. About their likings, their disliking and lots more.

Amreet: Anjana listen, most of our relatives were not in our marriage ceremony, so few of our relatives from the paternal side are also invited to this marriage. Purposefully, they are coming to meet you. So, try to handle them as best as possible. All of them have a conservative mind, so probably several things can run in their mind after seeing you. You don't be nervous seeing them.

Sure, you don't worry, Anjana replied politely.

CHAPTER SIX

Marriage Mania

Finally, they both arrived their destination.

Anjana could see the chaos that spread all over the house. The cluttering of people and giggling and chatting sound all over.

People were eagerly waiting to meet their "Choti Bahu" (younger daughter-in-law). Both the couple entered their house where Amreet's mom, dad and younger sister were eagerly waiting for them.

Bhabhi saying this his sister hugged Anjana. How are you?

I am good, you say, what's the feeling now? Nervous or excited? - Anjana teasingly asked

Bhabhi you na..... nanad (sister-in-law) sighs

Next day 7 AM

Anjana gets into the kitchen to prepare breakfast. Amreet is with his parents checking out what all are done and what else left.

Anjana, Anjana where are you?

I am in kitchen Amreet, what happen? Listen, we are supposed to leave for jewelry shopping. So. get ready fast.

They all left for the jewelry and dress shopping. Anjana was taking the responsibility of the amount for all these shopping. However, the shopping was almost done, suddenly.....

Amreet, I am not feeling well

What happen? Are you alright? Amreet asked nervously.

No, I am feeling vomiting and dizziness. Even my sight is getting blur. I am feeling very weakness.

The cluttering noise in the market was so much that Anjana had to struggle to transfer her voice to the Amreet.

Anyways, with the opinion of family members who were available there, both left for doctor.

Doctor: Yes, tell me

Anjana explains everything

The first statement that doctor gave was "Are you pregnant"?

With full of surety, Anjana replied "No sir"

Well, here's the medicine, take it. It's just a matter of weakness.

The date of ceremony was approaching, and the level of chaos was increasing day by day. You couldn't see anybody relaxing for even a single minute. Everyone seems in hurry.

Understanding her responsibility, Anjana engrossed herself in most of the work. Her time got minimized in kitchen and increased a lot in managing the bride's thing.

There were some members who were very happy with Anjana's responsibilities, while some others were also who were getting jealous as Anjana was caught up with maximum attention.

CHAPTER SEVEN

Unfolding Treasure of Happiness

Finally, the ceremony ended up happily and everyone was now back to their work. So, were Anjana and Amreet too. They both have to leave now because, Amreet's official leave was about to end and he was supposed to resume his office soon.

Due Amreet's tight schedule, he was bound to work late in his office. And, hence, Anjana has no other option then to leave alone in the house, watching Tv or working something.

Evening 7 PM

Anjana picks up her phone, dialed Amreet's number and...

Listen, I am not feeling well. Can you please come bit early

Amreet sounds worried, What happened?

I an having nausea feeling and dizziness.

I am on the way to home, but, still it will take more than 1 hour. You please lay on bed until I come.

Sure!

Next day morning 10 AM

------*Say Cheese, You're going to be a Daddy!*

It took a few second for him to process this big news

Amreet got a surprise of a lifetime, when his wife revealed that she was pregnant.

And why not? After all the mother-to-be however, shocked her husband with profound news of becoming a daddy.

Really?

Yes!

He hugged her instantly and cried with joy, It was the perfect moment and feeling that she will never forget.

Amreet holding her in his arm, "You have given me such a big surprise, trust me I am on cloud 9".

Yes, I can see that joy of being a father in your eyes Amrit.

Both of them hugged each other tightly.

Days passed on and Anjana's baby bumps were now becoming prominent, so was her level of tiredness. She could no more handle the household chores as efficiently as she could do before. It was just because the level of the hormonal changes in her body. The feeling of nausea and vomiting has now become the part and parcel of her life. She doesn't have the same eagerness and cravings towards the dishes as she had before. She gets agitated most of the time.

"A few days later they went to their first baby appointment and it was official that they in fact were going to have their first baby. Counting number of months/weeks being passed and still left has become the habit for them. Then it instantly became all about taking care of their little piece of love that was growing inside her. Finally, they made it to all the appointments.

In this situation, when Anjana was pregnant, she convinced Amreet to pursue MBA. This was just because, one day when they were somewhere out, Amreet revealed in front Anjana that once he wanted to do MBA. But, he wasn't able to complete after the first semester due to his hectic office schedule. At that point Anjana decided that she will go all the way long to support and help him in completing his degree.

She suggested to opt for the correspondence course and finally Amreet did. Now the tough time for Anjana has started. In spite of Amreet, she was studying, completing all assignments work, and many more. It was Anjana's 7th month going on when one night she was sitting on the stool and working on the Amreet's assignment. Amreet was sitting on the bed. Suddenly, one foot of the stool broke and Anjana fall down on floor. Luckily, her mind instructed her to hold the bedsheet which helped her not to fall down with maximum force. This might have hurted her baby inside the womb. But, unfortunately a minor pain raised on her left side of the stomach. Seeing this, Amreet got nervous and hastily picked her up. He quickly dialled up her gynae number and explained everything. He was asked to quickly rush to the nearby hospital to screen the stomach if baby was well. Amreet did the same.

As he reached the hospital, Anjana was taken inside the labor room and all her examinations were going on - Baby's heart-beat, pressure, etc. On the other hand, nurses and other hospital staffs were enquiring Amreet to know whether this accident was intentionally or unintentionally.

When eveything seems fine, Anjana was discharged from the hospital. On the way to home Amreet explained the matter that happed with him in hospital, and how he was under the doubt of hospital staffs about this accident.

CHAPTER EIGHT

Flip Side of Story- From An Author's Eye

When a girl is born in a family, the moment when her parents hold her in their arms, the first word that comes out from the heart is "Hamare ghar laxmi Aayi hai". Well, the word Laxmi (Wife of Lord Vishnu) is depicted to the Goddess who is a representative of health, wealth and prosperity of all forms. She is being nurtured and pampered by her parents with utmost care and where she never knows what does sacrifice means.

Gradually she starts growing up and yes, her first stage of sacrificing starts. If she is an elder sibling in the house, she has to make sacrifice in every aspect- Be it food, dresses, her toys as well as her playtimes. And if she is the younger one, she has to make sacrifice by waiting for her turn to come. No matter whether she is younger or older, but, the main subject is she is a "GIRL". This is the most important thing that she has to always grave in her mind.

Being a woman comes with number of expectations along with number of roles that she is expected to fulfill- As a single woman, as a daughter to her parents, as a sister to her siblings, as a wife to her husband and a daughter-in-law to her in-laws. Woman and Independence is completely metaphor to each other. Can a woman ever expect herself to do whatever she wants? Can she ever say "NO' with a full right without getting humiliated by her family members or being scrutinized by a society's giant microscope?

I Question Myself : Why Only Girls/ Women/Ladies?

Getting married is considered to be a milestone in one's life. Is this really right? Where on one hand it is a common saying that marriage is a unification of two different soul who are meant to take the responsibilities of each other. But, as much as I wonder over the years, it seems like it is only woman's responsibility. When people say relationships are always made in heaven. I really wonder if really relationships are made in heaven than definitely there shouldn't be any flaws in the relationship.

After marriage what girl expects, what are her expectations, what she sacrifices and what are the reality? I hope this book won't feel short for me to describe all these above in details.

CHAPTER NINE

Sacrifices, Expectations, Reality- Altogether Called Woman

Sacrifices: The biggest sacrifice that a girl makes is leaving her home where she was brought up for the past 25 years and moving to a new family where she has never ever been and accept that family as her own. When a girl leaves her parents and meet new parents in the form of in-laws, she takes them up as her own parents. Being a newly-wed, you will be treated nice as you are the epicentre of that family. But, as the days passes by, people keep on realizing you that you don't belong to that family. In every now and then faults, you will continuously be poked in such a way that you have attempted a crime and your parents are the one who have educated you the same. Without uttering any words, just tears roll down from her eyes. She starts missing her home, her family. But Alas, she can't even give them a call and let them know. Because she knew, doing this will not end up with any solution, but will deteriorate the reputation of her new family and will make her parents restless.

Every Girl May Not Be Queen To Her Husband, But, She Is Always a Princess to Her Father!

Expectations: Well, what should I say in terms of expectations. An understanding spouse is all that she wants. Days passes by! Anjana is now moved to a town with her husband. Both of them starts living as a nuclear family. Everything goes fine. Both seems very happy. Months on months passes very well when on one day, a conversation starts and all of a sudden, a normal conversation stretched up to such an extent, that she also lost her temper. And what shocked her was the abusive language from him.

Brought up in a middle-class family, she was never used to such languages. Those made her so disturbed that she doesn't know what to do. The only matter of discussion was that the girl has always expected to live a best lifestyle with her husband, she has dreamt a queen lifestyle and to get them fulfilled only by her hubby. But she was away from in-laws leaving a nuclear lifestyle. And that was only crime.

She knew that whatever she wanted, whatever she dreamt can only be fulfilled in a metro cities. She was never used to live in small town where people (People here I mean neighbors) are always eyeing on you, eyeing on your activities, eyeing just because you are a daughter-in-law and looking for one and other opportunity to poison one's ear. She was forced to settle down to a place where there were no one of her own. There were none with whom she could share her heart-felt feelings. Because, she knew that if she leaks anything from here, her secret won't be secret anymore. And hence, all these thoughts made her scared to settling there. But, whom should she say? If she utters any word, she will be bombarded with lots of blame and curse. Isn't that right of a married girl to live a happy and rich lifestyle with her husband? Is that something scandal? Then why people always try to cast an evil eye upon.

Well, on the other hand her in-laws always wanted to settle down both to the hometown. So, this was again a matter of issue. Every now and then, that girl was being realized that she was the one who has played a major role in creating a barrier between mother and son. She was made to realized that she is the only one who wants to live alone and take the leverage of the husband's salary alone.

While she was unmarried, her days has gone while in studies schooling from her hometown and further studies in the metro cities. She has likely got the time to stay at her home as she has to live outstation for jobs. This made her a slightly different from a common woman who held more proficiency in handling the household chores. But, let me tell you that being ambitious, that girl wasn't lame in terms of handling the household responsibilities. *Yes, her chappati wouldn't get round, but she was not less than others in terms of taking responsibilities.*

However, after her marriage she was bound to leave her job, because definitely she won't be able to give enough time to her family. But her inner ambition never ended. Six months after getting marriage, she started hunting for some freelance jobs. And as she was having good knowledge of market, hence, start receiving the work from home jobs. And hence, she laid her first step towards freelancing. Now, her life took another turn where apart from her day-to-day household chores, she was also in charge of work from home job.

How many of you agree with me that whether a woman goes to office or works from home, she is compelled to perform the responsibility towards household chores in the same pace. She has to carry usual chores and run errands around the house regardless of the time constraint. It is probably just because she is a girl or a Superwoman. Decision making and giving suggestions is another challenge where despite of knowing that something is going wrong to happen, she can't even give her suggestions or even if she managed to give, her suggestions will definitely be taken in a lighter way.

Reality: But the reality is somewhat different from the expectations. Most men wish not to part with their parent post marriage. Traditional, orthodox families expect their daughter-in-law to take the responsibility of the house and not to engrossed herself dedicately in career ambition. Spending money is also frowned upon as it seems that the girl is wasting the son's saving. Her each and every activity, no matter dressing up beautifully, wearing precious jewelries, dressing up with costly dresses delivers a message to in-laws that the girl is wasting my son's hard-earned money. But, on the other hand they believe that asking money from son, from brother or from uncle is a right for the family member.

CHAPTER TEN

Entry of a Cute Angel in a Couple's Life

Finally, after such a long wait time has arrived when a bunch of happiness was knocking at the door. Yes, it was the completion of 9 months of pregnancy and couple was ready to welcome a new family member anytime. Preparation has already started.

Anjana, I am a bit nervous how will we handle this situation alone?

"We must call both of our parents so that we can get both emotional support from them."

Yes Amreet, I guess you are right.

Amreet picked up his cell phone, dialed a number and ......

"Hello, didi, how are you? Listen, I have called you up to let you know that Anjan's delivery date is approaching. So, it would be helpful if you come over here."

Ok then, I will be booking your ticket. You be ready.

Call disconnected.

Shall we call Mummy, Papa also? (Anjana's Mom and dad)

"Sure, why not", Anjana replied with joy. After all, who girl doesn't like to take the opportunity to spend time with her parents.

Amreet picked up the phone again, dialed Anjan's dad's number, and...

Papa, namaste, hope everything is good. I was thinking that it would be good if you and mummy come here and take care of Anjana during delivery time.

Anjana was overwhelmed with joy. And why not, after all preparation has been started to welcome their new baby.

The next day morning, Anjana got a call from her mom.

Beta, when is the expected delivery date?

"It can be any day in the second week"... Anjana replied!

Ok, we are booking the ticket and will be there on the 13th of October. Mom said.

Sure maa.

10th of October, door bell rang.....

Anjana opened the door, It was Amrit with his elder sister. (Amreet went railway station to receive his didi)

Namaste didi, please come inside.

How are you, Amreet's sister asked Anjana

I am good by God's grace. Refreshen yourself, and have something.

(Let me tell you that in this situation, Anjana was only one who was in charge of preparing food, washing utensils, and doing other household chores.)

Anjana's level of restlessness was increasing day by day. She couldn't get peaceful sleep during the night, but still, she has to wake up in the morning to prepare breakfast and lunch for Amrit.

Nothing changed in her work level despite of increasing one member in the family.

12th of October - It was the day when her parents were arriving. She was very excited.

"Hello Amreet, where are you? Did you find papa"?

Yes, yes, they have already arrived and are now in my car.

It will take another 45 mins to reach home... Amrit replied.

Ohh, come fast.

Finally, Amreet was on the door with Anjana's parents.

The house now was full of guests with lots of chaos and chirping.

Lots of discussions, unlimited planning, etc were being discussed with each other.

However, Anjana's mother has taken the kitchen responsibility, while her dad took the responsibility of cleaning. (This was just because, they don't want their daughter to get tired at this stage. After all, that's why a parent has been given the place next to God)

But, alas, in such a happening situation, there was someone who wanted to create controversy among Amrit and his in-laws (Anjana's parents). Every now and then something and other was being transferred into Amrit's ears that was enough to make him agitated.

12th October, night 11 PM, after having dinner together, Anjana started feeling restless. She was neither able to sit properly nor stand. And something happened that made her nervous. Yes, water break, which means baby can get delivered anytime.

She straight forward went to the bed and laid beside Amreet..

Tears rolling down her eyes...

What happen Anjana, tell me. Are you ok?

No Amreet. I had a water break just now. I am feeling very nervous.

The moment when she uttered this statement made Amreet fidgety. He hastily got up and said... We need to rush hospital right now.

From another room, Anjana's mother came and asked, what happen Amreet?

Mummy, we need to go to the hospital and admit Anjana right now. Didi, you pack Anjana's bag... Amrit screamed...

Amreet holds Anjana and carefully got down the stairs towards the car. Mom, Dad and didi accompanied him.

Finally, they reached the hospital and Anjana was taken under the care of doctors and nurses.

Further medication process starts

Amreet and Anjana's dad were waiting outside the labor room, while her mom and didi were with Anjana. They were waiting to get the labor pain, as there was no pain till now.

Finally, at 3 AM in the morning, Anjana's labor pain started. It was getting unbearable from time to time. but, hats off to her. She was such strong that she neither screamed nor showed any haste. She bore the pain with only her tears rolling down her eyes.

With unbearable pain, she was lying down for the next 15 hrs and finally, the joyous moment has arrived when she gave birth to a baby boy.

Then the day finally came. After a whole night at the hospital at 5.03 PM on 14th October, 2017 Aayan was born.

That day and that moment was the most cherishable moment in their life. But, as every coin has its flip side, similarly every moment has happiness adhered with the worst situation too. Certain situation occured that made Anjana traumatised for several months.

Seeing her little angel, all her pain vanished and she couldn't control herself seeing her son at first sight.

On the other side, everyone was waiting outside eyeing the door of the operation theatre to get open.

The door opened, a stature pushed by 4 people was coming out of the room, and guess what, it was Anjana lying on it, completely unconscious, tired, and weak.

After few hours when she was able to respond and identify everyone, Amreet was in front of her with a smile on his face.

Congratulations, Amrit said rolling his hand over her head.

Anjana can feel the level of peace the moment she felt the loving hand of Amreet on her head.

CHAPTER ELEVEN

Shattering Happiness in a Moment

Anjana was lying in the hospital bed when a paediatrician visited her asking for the baby's daddy.

Hello mam, Can I see the father of the baby?

Sir, he has left for home, please tell me what has happened... Anjana replied

We have kept your baby in neonatal ICU under observation. The baby is suffering from jaundice. Though, it's just a normal case, but still we need to monitor it very closely.

Hearing this, Anjana got speechless. She immediately called up Amrit and....

Amreet, please come to the hospital immediately. (Anjana sobbing).

Yes, I am on the way. What happened? Does the doctor come for visit?

Yes, he said that there are some complications with our baby. Please come first. I am getting nervous.

Within half an hour, Amreet was in the hospital. He immediately went to the doctor and discussed each and everything.

Don't worry, everything is fine... Amreet convinced Anjana.

But, Anjana could see tension reflecting clear from his face.

The next day morning, the gynaecologist visited Anjana's ward to make a routine check-up. After monitoring each and everything..

Doctor: Anjana, how are you feeling?

Better mam.

That's good.

I am writing few medicines as well as few exercises that you need to perform on daily basis.

You are now fine to get a discharge.

Thanks, Mam... Anjana silently said.

On one end she was happy that it's time to go home, but, on the other end, she was worried because she has to leave her baby in NICU. What to do, there was no other option too.

Amreet completed the entire discharging formalities and took Anjana carefully home.

Unaware of everything that has happened till date while she was in the hospital, she was waiting for a warm welcome. But nothing has happened like that.

As soon as she entered the house, her mom was ready with a hot water bucket and clothes to bathe her daughter.

After getting a bath, she had her lunch and lie down on the bed. But, one thing that was hitting in her mind was the crying face of her mom. She could sense something fishy has happened in her absence, but, didn't utter any words understanding the call of an hour.

Let me give you a massage... asking this mom pulled Anjana's leg and started applying oil.

Amreet was also tired and sitting next to Anjana.

Bhai, I need to go to the same gynaecologist from whom Anjana was getting treatment. Amreet's sister said.

What's that? Anjana thought... Just now we have arrived home from the hospital and she is asking Amreet to take her to the doctor. What so urgency that she can't even wait for one to two days?

And if it was so urgent, then she could have called her husband to take her for treatment. Why expecting from brother to involve in the woman's matter? This thought made Anjana feel irritated. However, there was no choice so, she has to shut her mouth.

Finally, both brother and sister left for a doctor......

[*How do you feel when you as a patient arrive and someone from your in-law's side wants to draw all the attention towards herself, despite knowing that it's not the right time to raise any personal issues in a situation when both husband and wife has just returned from such a big surgery.*]

Days passed by, and Amreet kept on visiting the hospital to have a glance at his baby. He never missed the opportunity to meet him. While going to the office, he first used to visit his son, whisper in his ears, talk with him and when meeting time gets over, he used to leave for office.

This routine was repeated every day, and now the baby can even sense his father. One morning when Amreet after completion of hospital visiting hours was on his way to the office, he got a call from the hospital.

Rrrrrr....... phone bell rings

Hello.. Amreet picked

Sir, your baby is crying so much. Please come.

Hearing this Amreet made a U-turn and reached the hospital. He went close to the baby and whispered something in his ears that made him stop crying.

Nurses in NICU around were shocked as to what did father whispered in the baby's ears that made him quiet.

Sometimes Anjana has to go to the hospital for feeding her baby. And this happened regularly.

Till then, everything was fine. When one day Anjana got a call that baby needs to feed. So, she along with her mom and sister-in-law left for the hospital. As soon as she reached, she could find that still there was time for entry, so she thought in the meantime why not buy some snacks for mom and her in-law. She bought tea and namkeen for both of them, but, didn't have anything as she was not willing to.

All of them then entered the hospital and reached near the NICU. Anjana went inside and took her baby in her lap and started feeding. As soon as he felt asleep, she came outside and sat on a bench. All of a sudden, she started feeling dizziness. She called

Amreet and...

Amreet, please bring something to eat, I am not feeling well.

Yeah, just reached the hospital. I am buying something from the canteen. You rest in the meantime.

Hastily, Amreet arrived with some snacks and buns in his hand. He nervously asked his sister, Didi, Anjana didn't have anything till now?

And guess what his sister replied... Arey bhai, just now she had tea and snacks, and I only bought for both of them.

Hearing this lie shocked Anjana...

Anyways, Anjana had snacks and lay there for a while and finally, they all came back home.

This was the first step laid by Anjana's sister-in-law to start the battle.

And something happened that she never expected.

She has poised his brother's ear so much that the attitude of Amreet for Mom and dad has also changed. Both brother and sister created chaos in the family so much that even Anjana's mom dad couldn't keep themselves silent, and why not. It was now upon their self-respect. The scenario got worst so much that mom dad finally decided to leave the home in night itself, without seeing their grandson.

The battle which was being prepared every day by Amreet's sister ended up finally making Anjana's parents forcefully leaving the home.

However, things didn't end up here. Amreet's sister was so cunning that she knew that as Anjana's parents are not there so, the entire responsibilities of work will be on her head. Hence, next day she called her husband and went to stay with him. And finally after staying for 2-3 days with her husband she left for her hometown.

CHAPTER TWELVE

Flashback of the Anjana's and Amreet's Discussion Before Marriage

Before starting any new chapter, let me take you all to the flashback when Anjana and Amreet used to meet and discuss much more about the family as well as their upcoming marriage life...

Amreet: While on the way to dropping Anjana at her PG...

Anjana, see there is a lot of expectations in my family from choti bahu.

Anjana: Like?

Actually, Maa is not happy with bhabhi (Brother-in-law's wife). She doesn't even take care of her. Not even she asks her for food. Bhabhi lives only according to her wishes. She is not at all bothered of anyone. Maa desperately wants a daughter, not daughter-in-law who always sits beside her, gossiping and never letting her feel lonely.

Anjana: Oh, that's very bad of bhabhi. This attitude is really not good. Don't worry Amrit. I will always take care of her and will try to become a good daughter-in-law, unlike bhabhi.

Amreet (kissing her forehead)- Thanks dear!

....

It has been 3 years of marriage and things that were all blur till date were getting cleared day by day. Anjana was now well aware of the fact that it was not bhabhi, but only her mother-in-law who always tried playing games against her. And now the same has started happening with her. Things were getting so messy day by day that she started realizing that it was her biggest fault for choosing to marry Amreet. She could have denied that day itself when Amreet's family asked for dowry. She could now get the flashback of her father's face who for the first time felt so helpless when he was asked for a hefty amount as a dowry. Not only that, one day before marriage he was being called by Amreet's brother to send the rest of the amount or else the marriage was not going to happen.

"Imagine a situation of a father whose daughter is getting married and he has the pressure of delivering the rest of the amount to her in-law's house."

The statement made Anjana's dad a bit agitated but, calmly he handled the situation saying that the amount is already ready. The next day when you arrive with the groom, I'll be handling the amount.

The situation was in hand now, and they all agreed with the same. But something that was going in Anjana's mind was that "Am I doing something wrong marrying Amreet? Am I wrong in judging the guy?"

However, there was no choice left, so everything happened as it was planned.

CHAPTER THIRTEEN

The Real Face of Anjana's In-laws

Days, Months, and Years passed by. Things were not as smooth as they seemed to be. The level of worries for Anjana was increasing day by day. And one day something happened that she was never ready to accept it.

While she was cleaning old things from the bed box, she found some greeting cards with some romantic notes on them. However, she already knew that Amreet was having a girlfriend before marriage, but that hardly made her worried much because it was all before her marriage. but, one day when she opened his facebook account, she found that both of them has chatted together even after their marriage. This made her very much agitated.

One night, after Amreet was back to home from office-

Anjana: Amreet, Are you still in touch with that girl, Neha?

Amreet: Who?

Anjana: You better know about whom I am talking

Amreet in a hard voice: That means you are spying on me always? Anjana, see I don't like all these activities.

Anjana (in anger): Great Amreet, how could you say so calmly after doing all this. What would be your reaction if I would have done the same? And moreover, not only you, but even your family would have started cursing me and my family, isn't it? That means if a boy does wrong, hardly matters. But, if a girl is wrong, she and her family would be dragged in a bad manner.

I have already told you earlier that it doesn't bother me anything whatever you have done before marriage. But, after marriage, I won't accept all these nuisances. Understood? - Anjana repeated

The next day morning, when Amreet was getting ready for the office, his cell phone was ringing continuously. When he came out of the bathroom, Anjana asked,

Whose call is coming again and again?

Amreet: From office

Anjana: Is it? I am noticing that every day at the same time you get a call from this number. Swear on me that this is not the same girl.

Amreet: Completely silent.

Finally, he left for office.

In the afternoon, Anjana's phone rang. She was in the kitchen preparing lunch for herself. Wondering that her mom has called, she rushed from the kitchen towards the bedroom. But when she picked up the cell phone, she found that it was Amreet.

Anjana received the call: Yes, tell me (In anger)

Amreet: See, I have called up and told her that we won't be in a relationship anymore. I can't talk to you. My marriage life is ruining.

Anjana (in a sarcastic way): Ohh is it? Great. But, why did you call her in my absence? So, I don't trust you whatever you say. Do whatever you want. Saying this Anjana disconnected the call.

But she was completely disturbed.

The same night when Amreet was sleeping, Anjana was feeling restless. She picked up Amreet's phone slowly and blocked that Neha's number. Even from the social media account, she blocked her.

....

After few days Anjana and Amreet were supposed to go to their hometown. Because Amreet's mom wanted to spend some time with Aayan (son of Amreet and Anjana). This time Anjana was supposed to stay for a month.

But something that was making her worry was that in her absence, Amreet might call Neha.

One day when Anjana was sitting in the balcony in Amreet's parents' house, all of a sudden, his sister said, "Anjana, do you know Amreet has lots of friends, in fact girlfriends." Anjana just stared at her but didn't reply anything. His sister further added, before your married we went to Amreet place and there he met us that girl. She was nice and we were all ready with the proposal, but her family doesn't want to accept it. On this Amreet's mother who was also hearing this smiled gently. This statement hurted a lot to Anjana, but she never disclosed the same in front of Amreet.

One thing that was continuously running in her mind was that, "Is this the reason why mother-in-law is always teasing and cursing me." Why she always kept on telling me that, "What have you brought with you from your parent's place? Your father hadn't given us any dowry."

These thoughts have started sowing the seed of hatred in the heart of Anjana against her in-laws.

One month passed, and finally, a day has come when Amreet was coming to take Anjana back. She was so excited that after one month she was going to meet her hubby. Lots of preparation of dishes as well as she dressed up nicely to welcome him.

Anjana wasn't aware that Amreet has arrived because she was busy in the kitchen. Amreet straight forward went to the kitchen to meet her. Both of them were so glad to see each other and hugged together. Amreet then had breakfast and sat to gossip with his mom.

Anjana checked Amreet's phone whether the number was unblocked or still blocked. The thing that surprised her was that number was in the unblocked condition. She straightforward called Amreet in room asked the reason.

Anjana: you again called her in my absence.

Amreet: No Anjana, I didn't

Anjana: Don't lie Amreet. Then why you have unblocked the number?

Amreet: Mmmmm, Actually, she called me up for some job opportunities. That's why.

Anjana: That's great. You will never change Amreet. You are really disgusting

Things were getting complicated day by day for Anjana. For some or other reasons, they both start fighting. And the most tragic thing was that her in-laws were also ready to poison the ears of his son.

The worst part of Amreet's parents was that whenever Anjana desires to go and meet her parents, they were always ready to oppose. Not only Anjana but, the same happens with her bhabhi. Anjana was so disturbed seeing all these, because, her sisters-in-law were always visiting her parents now and then, but she was not at all allowed to go to her parent's house. And if by chance she would get the opportunity, Amreet's parents never let her go happily. For some or other reasons they would create a rivalry scene in the home.

One day on a very special occasion, Amreet has invited his sisters along with their in-laws. So Anjana and her brother-in-law wife were together preparing variety of dishes.

Bhabhi: Please take care of mutton, I am preparing biryani.

Anjana: Sure Bhabhi!

Though, Anjana was good at cooking, but, whenever she goes her in-law's place, her cooking style gets worst. It may be due to the mental pressure of her in-laws or something else, but it happens most of the time. The same happened that day. The mutton kebab which she was supposed to prepare got worse than she ever expected.

And later what happened with Anjana was really unexpected.

In the evening when guests went away, the entire family was sitting in the corridor. No not for gossiping, but for scolding her to such an extent that hardly any girl can bear it. Everyone including Amreet was scolding Anjana as if she has done some major crime that can't be excused. And as usual her parents were being dragged in the mid, their culture, and the way they have grown her.

(Let me ask the reader, is it the way a person should be insulted and only for such a minor and common mistake that can be

happened with anyone? If this is something that a girl after the marriage has to suffer or also sees getting her parents being insulted, then why do parents think about marrying a girl? Why not parents think about the aftermath effect of the marriage and let the girl stay at home happily? Why not reject the marriage on the face itself when a guy's parents ask for dowry? Why not file a complaint against them despite knowing that asking for dowry is a crime?)

CHAPTER FOURTEEN

Backbiting, A Special Talent!

However, this has just become a habit for her in-laws. Scolding, cursing, always making her insult, etc was just a common phenomenon for them. Maybe just because their upbringings were in this way only. Because a well-cultured and educated family will never try to insult their daughter-in-law for any minimal faults. Backbiting was again a special talent in them. They never dare to say anything on the face especially on Anjana's face. Whatever fault of her they wanted to count, they gossip either to their elder daughter-in-law or their son, and anything about elder daughter-in-law they used to gossip to the younger son.

One day something happened that kept Anjana traumatised.

While returning back from in-laws place, Amreet got a call in train..

Amreet: Yes, yes sure... No Problem

Anjana: Who's this?

Amreet: Sister called me up..(Younger sister)

Anjana: [*With an irritating voice*] *Why what happened?*

Amreet: Actually, her husband is also coming back, so, she was saying that it would be good if he could stay with you for few days.

Anjana: Tell him "No". I am not at all going to serve him. (*Actually, Anjana was angry on her in-laws and Amreet. Because according to them, she was worth for nothing.) So, she decided that she will not become servant for anyone anymore. If no one can give respect to her, then they have no rights to take respect from her.*

Hearing this, Amreet got angry and picked up his cell phone, dialed a number and....

"Don't let your husband visit to my place".

Imagine, both the couple has just arrived from hometown. Tired, restless, but were fighting for some useless reason which hardly matters for them at all.

Both of them reached to their flat. Without uttering a single word, Amreet took bath, change dress and left for his office.

Anjana also got herself engaged in cleaning the mess. Unaware of everything, she got a call from her mom.

Yes mom, how are you?

Mom on the other side of call: Anjana tell me the truth what has happened with you?

Anjana: Nothing mom, hiding her tears, but, with heavy voice.

Mom: Anjana, Amreet has called me up and said so many things. You are my daughter, and I want to hear from you..

Anjana (sobbing): (*She has never ever disclosed anything whatever she was facing at her in-law's place. But, when she got to know that Amreet has told everything, she can't control herself.*) Crying vigorously, she said each and everything she had faced till date. She revealed what Amreet's parents has done with her and how was Amreet treating.

Hearing this Anjana's mom felt very bad for her daughter. But her father got so angry that he wanted to call Amreet's parents and talk to them directly. But, Anjana stopped them.

Anjana now called Amreet.

Anjana: You stupid fellow, you think that you have acted smartly with me. Oh, I must say thank you for this cheap and rubbish activity. Till now you use to blackmail me that you will call my parents and say everything. But I used to stop you and get scared that what if you call them. But now you have cleared my route by yourself. You have encouraged me to utter each and every activity of you and your parents to my family. Thanks to you again.

Saying this Anjana disconnected the call.

CHAPTER FIFTEEN

Visit of In-Laws to the Couple's Place

Almost some three years of their marriage, but no one from Amreet's place has visited the couple's house without any reasons. It may either be for the job's purpose or for treatment, those who came has some or other reasons. However, Anjana always wanted that family members from Amreet's place must visit to her house and see how these couple were living and managing everything alone. So, she has always asked her mother-in-law and father-in-law to visit their place.

Hence, a time has come when Amreet's mom and dad has decided to visit the place where their son and daughter-in-law were residing. Hearing this, both were very excited and engrossed themselves in making preparations. Amreet has booked their train ticket and instructed each and everything, as this was the first time when his parents were coming alone in the train. Finally, a day has come when they were arriving. Anjana woke up in the morning and..

Anjana: Amreet there are certain kitchen things that I require. Make sure that you purchase everything before you leave for the station.

Amreet: Arey, don't worry. Their train will reach in the evening. So, there is enough time. By that time, I will bring everything what all you require.

Anjana: Yes please, make sure that you bring everything as early as possible so that I can complete preparing food on time.

Anjana was confused what to make. Whether she should make non-veg or something simple. Struggling herself in thinking, she finally decided to make something simple along with some sweet dish.

Evening 4 o'clock, Amreet has left with his car to pick up his parents from railway station.

Anjana: Where did you reach?

Amreet? I have already picked them up. But, a great problem..

Anjana: What happened Amreet? Speak up clearly..

Amreet: Maa is continuously vomiting. Her condition is getting worst. And on the other hand, this irritating traffic... I really don't know what to do?

Anjana: Ohh...

Doorbell rings...

Anjana opens the door. She could see her mother-in-law is very bad situation, lethargic, tired, standing with support of father-in-law on one side and Amreet on the other side.

Anyhow they came inside and made her lie in bed.

She was not even in the situation that she could sit and have at least a sip of water.

Anjana sat beside her and asked..

Maa how are you feeling?

(with a very low voice) I am not at all feeling well. Everything seems moving.

Anjana brought a glass of lemon water and asked her to drink sip by sip. Then she slowly slowly rolled her hand over her back to make her feel better.

Anjana could see that her mother-in-law was trying to fall asleep. So, she got up and went straight in the kitchen to make some arrangement for her father-in-law. She arranged plates with dishes and made him to eat. All have a good time together talking, discussing and giggling.

Days passed by. Both the couple has already planned for an outing with them. So, all of them were very excited to go for outing. They had a very special time clicking selfies, photos and roaming here and there at a very new place.

One day when Anjana, Amreet and his mom dad were somewhere out just to buy some groceries item, Anjana got a call from her mom.

Mom on the other side of the call: Anjana, beta how are you?

Anjana: I am good mom. How is Gracy and her baby?

Both of them are good. But, Gracy is bit depressed. Her health is not that perfect....

Anjana continued talking to her mom without having an idea that there was someone in the car who was continuously keeping her ears on their talk. After the conversation got over and call got disconnected, Anjana suddenly started feeling dizziness. So, as soon as they arrive home, without uttering a single word, Anjana straight forward went to her room and lie down.

Seeing that, her mom-in-law asked her to prepare food. Among four members of the family, neither three of the members (father-in-law, mother-in-law and Amreet) bothered to ask Anjana what has happened. Hearing that she was called up to prepare dinner, Anjana woke up and went to the kitchen. She cut the veggies and prepared the dishes. Her mind was not working at all and not allowing her to think what she was preparing and how. Unfortunately, when the food was served, Amreet shouted on her asking that 'Is this the way you should cook vegetable?

Anjana: Amreet, please don't shout. I am not well. And really, I didn't do anything intentionally.

Amreet: Taste it. You have intentionally poured jar of salt in it.

Anjana: No Amreet, I have not done this intentionally (Anjana sobbing).

Mother-in-law: As soon as she got the chance of pouring ghee in fire, she leaped herself ahead to ignite the Amreet's anger. Arey beta, you don't know what happened. Actualy her mother has said something and poised her ears that she is showing her drama to us,

Amreet's mother said.

Father-in-law: In villages, woman like you must be beaten and should have burnt her face with hot tawa. Call her parents and ask them to come over here. We need to make final decision one on one.

Amreet: Yes dad, you are right. I must call them.

All these violent talks made Anjana helpless and alone. She felt so lonely that she wasn't able to explain how she was feeling.

She however managed to pass whole night thinking that marrying Amreet was the biggest mistake she has done in her entire life.

Finally, one day Amreet's parents wanted to leave for their hometown. So, they asked him to book ticket for them. And the day has come when they were leaving. Amreet and Anjana both went to see off them.

Three of four days has passed when Amreet's parents have left, Amreet's health was getting deteriorated. He was getting depressed day by day. His interest from everything was going off. Neither he gets hungry, nor has the willing in anything. He neither gets sleep whole night. Seeing her husband disturbed due to anxiety and depression, she started to counsel him most of the time. She used to feed him with her own hands, make dishes in which his interest was and do whatever she could do.

One day when Amreet was sitting and watching television, Anjana came and sat beside him. She said Amreet, how do you feel, please explain me clearly.

Amreet: Anjana, I really don't know, but sometimes I feel that something will happen with me. I will die and etc. etc.

Anjana: Do you feel like crying?

Amreet: Yes!

Anjana: Then why do you feel shy. Cry out loud. Take out all your emotions out. Cry in front of me as much as you want. I am your wife and I must help you in every situation you pass by.

Hearing thing, Amreet couldn't control himself and hugged Anjana with his tears in her eyes. Holding him tight, Anjana said, cry Amreet. Cry as much as you feel..

Finally, Amreet felt relaxed. wipe out his tears and said. Anjana, I am feeling better now.

Anjana: Amreet, it was the same situation that day as you are feeling now. But you, your mom and dad showered uncountable bitter words on me. No one bothered to pamper me and ask how I was feeling that day. Even you as a husband was not by my side. I felt so lonely Amreet, that I can't explain.

Now, see how helpless you are feeling. But, I am always here to make you comfortable.

Amreet (feeling guilty): I am extremely sorry Anjana for what I did. I am really feeling guilty for myself.